ALL THAT JAZZ

Gerry Boland

ALL THAT JAZZ

All that Jazz

is published in 2022 by
ARLEN HOUSE
42 Grange Abbey Road
Baldoyle
Dublin D13 A0F3
Ireland
Email: arlenhouse@gmail.com
www.arlenhouse.ie

ISBN 978–1–85132–292–3, paperback

International distribution:
SYRACUSE UNIVERSITY PRESS
621 Skytop Road, Suite 110
Syracuse
New York 13244–5290
USA
Email: supress@syr.edu
www.syracuseuniversitypress.syr.edu

© Gerry Boland, 2022

The moral right of the author has been asserted

Typesetting by Arlen House

cover images: 'Sanctum' and 'Meditation V'
by Jacinta O'Reilly
are reproduced courtesy of the artist
www.jacintaoreilly.com

Contents

- 9   The Dog, the Accordion and the Stars
- 10   The Poem and the Blackbird
- 11   Fourteen Oyster Catchers
- 12   Rosses Point
- 13   Lissadell
- 14   The Day After the Rain
- 15   Photograph
- 17   Meeting You Again
- 18   April in Strandhill
- 19   Red Stockings
- 20   Instructions on How to Fall in Love
- 22   Blossoms
- 23   Driving to my Lover
- 24   Faith
- 25   Absence
- 26   Six Swans
- 27   Snow in Paris
- 28   Remembering Palermo
- 29   Had I Been Listening
- 30   Trust
- 32   What he Usually Did
- 33   Murphy's Law
- 34   Letting Go
- 35   Stupid
- 36   Elements
- 37   Spinning
- 38   The Poems I Write Now
- 39   Looking Back
- 40   Picture This
- 41   Warrior of the Heart
- 44   Winter's Arrival
- 45   Connections

46	Glove
47	Mid-Points
48	The Things they Say
49	On My 10th Birthday
50	Those Wives
51	His Women
52	Poetry and Physiotherapy
53	Artifice
54	Silent
55	The Competition
56	This Foolishness
57	When All is Said and Done
58	Ailbhe
59	16th October
60	Inner City
61	Casablanca
62	The Master
63	Ring
64	Freedom
65	Lockdown
66	*Acknowledgements*
67	*About the Author*

ALL THAT JAZZ

THE DOG, THE ACCORDION AND THE STARS
i.m. Dermot Healy

The dog whines.
She doesn't understand
what has come over me
now that I've been outside

and back in.
She cannot see the stars
I have brought with me
into the small room.

She beats her tail
on the linoleum.
Jackie Daly's accordion
keeps time.

When I close my eyes
I can follow the road
from Ballyconnell to Finea
by the stars in my head.

They are my guide
to wherever I choose to go.
The accordion tilts the moon
back to Sheelin and Kinale.

The dog's tail goes still.

The Poem and the Blackbird

There is a reason I sit here,
just after dawn, a pen in my hand,
the blank page waiting

for my elusive, inner world
to reveal itself in an unexpected phrase,
or a startling, remarkable thought –

like the one that comes to me now,
a thought so profound
it causes me to leave down my pen,

walk to the door and open it,
listen to what the blackbird has to say
this early March morning.

Fourteen Oyster Catchers

He drove to Streedagh Strand,
thought he might get a poem out of it,
the winter morning wet and misty,
ideal for composing.

He met a man who talked and could not stop.
A poem was out of the question.
Keeping up with the monologue was a job in itself.
And so he walked, and listened, and nodded,

and as one long, rambling tale
moved seamlessly on to the next,
he watched fourteen oyster catchers
take to the air and fly into the mist.

Rosses Point

Rosses Point is where we go when the earth has turned
and winter weakens its grip.
Once more, we fool ourselves that all will be fine.

The beach's gentle curve, terns clustered on the shoreline,
a cormorant skimming the flat sea, and there, rising as one
to the dog's bark, a flock of geese above the brine.

We step upon the damp sand. The air, already clearing
winter's congestion, feels soft on our cheeks,
like the gentle caress of a mother's hand,

or the touch of a god we've barely known.

LISSADELL

That was an odd sort of summer.
Hard to remember now what we did,
how we put in the time.

There was a visit to Lissadell,
I remember that, the two of us
basking in the sun in the courtyard,

drinking coffee,
sharing intimacies
in our early-days testing of the waters.

You took out your phone,
showed me photos of your family:
a mother, a brother, two sisters.

I gave you a potted history of mine,
your eyes widening with each new sibling.
You said you couldn't wait to meet them.

That was the week of the sun, when it felt
as if the summer was only just beginning,
and we set sail into a clear blue sky.

The Day After the Rain

The day after the rain
and a dense grey quilt hangs
over the sullen Connaught town.

The river is in a frenzy.
It cascades under the old stone bridge,
ferries odd tokens from the uplands.

This, for instance: a battered handbag
snagged on the bough of a snapped alder,
its precious contents long gone,

except for one trapped gem,
a gleaming pearl,
polished by the currents,

winking at the riverbank,
a memento of a moment in time
before it all turned sour,

when expectations were high,
when hope was in the ascendant,
when things, against the odds, were looking up.

Photograph

Forgive me the frailty of my memory,
I know I should remember you better.

Was there something in the air,
or were we simply friends for a while?

Could we, *should* we, have embraced?
Would anything have come of it, do you think?

You were awkward and I was shy,
no argument there.

All I have to remember you by
is this photograph I hold in my hand –

you, taken by me, back in '93,
February, near Kiladoon, County Mayo.

Barefooted, you paddle towards me,
jeans rolled to your kneecaps,

black shoes in your right hand,
your left stuffed into the pocket of your jacket.

You are looking at me and you are laughing
and now I remember what a lovely face you had.

I was with another then,
which would explain your distance,

if that is what you were doing,
maintaining a distance.

Or maybe you were game and I wasn't, simple as that.

Or, that I was game and you were not. That, too.

Meeting You Again

You are driving home now
after our brief encounter on a busy street,
back across the country,
to your husband, to your children,

and I'm remembering
the first time we met
in that old drawing room,
how you stood on the carpet

in your yellow cotton dress,
your arms touching your sides,
your unblinking, blue, amazed eyes
while I jabbered on –

and what I liked was the way
you were no one else but you.
I guess I fell in love with you then,
which happens,

it happens all the time.
Mostly there is no place or space
for this tiny seed of love to grow
and so it dies before it can bloom.

Ours was this kind of love.
We met, we leaned in,
we thought we might,
we leaned away again.

You are driving home now,
leaving us both a little stunned
by what has happened,
though mostly by what did not.

April in Strandhill

This could be summer, here at Strandhill.
Teenage boys and teenage girls, in t-shirts and shorts,
drinking beer and smoothies under a warm sun,
talking, laughing, laughing, talking.

These early April days are scarcely believable,
they will spoil the coming months
with their false promise of hope and happiness.
It cannot last, this much we know.

The warrior crow knows what's what.
Brazenly perched on a vacated table,
she seems to think she owns this seaside caff.
Truly she is in her scavenger element,

as I am, watching the oh so young waitress
jaunt here, then there, back to here.
I turn away, away from all that jazz;
my summers have all run their course.

Red Stockings

Fetching, that's what he says to her,
because he can, because she is with child,
because he is spoken for, because there are no possibilities.

Red stockings below a black dress
unhinge him for the day,
those much dwelled upon legs
wandering the long corridors,
supporting her near full-term treasure.

It may have nothing to do with sex. It may be all about sex.
In the end it doesn't matter, yet today it is a tsunami
flooding through his body,

flushing out every last good intention,
each one a brick in a wall he's built around him,
locking him in, shutting him down.

Instructions on How to Fall in Love

It's simple
just follow these rules

leave your ego on a shelf
better still lock it in a drawer

abandon the house and walk
through meadows flashing
tall grass and meadowsweet
Common Blues and Small Coppers
tumbling in and out of view

wander along an ancient lane
with gentle turns and uncut hedges
and birds singing their tiny hearts out

all this must take place in early June
there should be a stillness in the air
and a sense that paradise is within reach

find a tall tree
lean your back against it
tell it you have fallen in love
that this feeling of love
has no boundaries

linger here until you feel
the tree loves you back
for the secret of love
is only dawning on you now

return to the sacred place
you call home
go about your daily business

it will not be long
before someone sees
you are open for love

when she presents herself
you will know.

Blossoms

It gives me little pleasure to recall
those mornings when you would call
to me to rise, to come and see
the blossoms on the apple tree

that you had planted that first year
to celebrate what was always clear,
my heart being then so close to you,
our love, as in the song, so true.

There's someone else I live for now;
a love that mirrors the ancient vow
we made while under siege from shrill warnings
that infiltrated our stolen mornings.

We held fast, love, we stood our ground,
we always knew what we had found
would hold steady, would see us through:
for love *was* strong, love *was* true.

Driving to My Lover

It's been a while,
there is catching up to do –

and more: love to be made, perhaps,
if we can manage it on the back streets of Mullingar.

I dressed for the occasion, prepared a packed lunch for two,
brushed my thick, handsome hair.

She will consider this day an adventure,
a chance to get away, to entertain this old notion,

retest the waters, try us on once more
for comfort and reliability.

Let's go with the flow is what I think I'll say.
Let's see where the current takes us

this time.

Faith

How it is that we found each other I will never know.
Randomness, I guess,

unless there is a higher power at work,
an idea that might find favour with you,

though not with me, who believes in
what I know and what I see and what I hear

and none of that miracle stuff.
I have faith in you but in little else,

faith that you will remain faithful –
until the day I might let you down so badly

you would cut me out of your life –
now here, now gone.

In a previous life this could well have happened,
but I am a new man now, unrecognisable from the man

you woke from a dream that made no sense,
least of all to himself.

ABSENCE

I have come back to you and you are unchanged,
your constant self here, and I take hold of you.

The long days and nights without you
have taken a heavy toll.

Your arms enfold me, your long hair
falls across your face, our cheeks touch,

and I find myself wondering what it was all about,
why I put us through this separation,

when at the end of it I see it is you who are unchanged,
perhaps stronger, and I a little weaker than before.

I make a vow, in the hallway, our arms
holding each other in a tight embrace:

I will not leave you again I say,
and you know I never will.

Six Swans

Six swans are flying low over Market Yard,
honking, like long-distance lorries,
waking me from my stupor,
from the dense fog of battle in my head.
I have left you where I last saw you,
a little bewildered I suspect
in the wake of my silence,
my out-of-the-blue darkness.
From nowhere it came and,
like a stray dog, it has retreated.

The six low-flying swans
cross the Shannon at Ging's Pub,
announcing their passage,
their enormous wings batting down the air,
their sonorous honks an ancient tonic.
I am on my way back
to where I abandoned you,
to tell you about the swans,
how six of them flew over Market Yard,
how sorry I am that you did not see them.

Snow in Paris

Paris,
silenced by twelve hours of snow,
got under my skin,
the houses and gardens transformed,
the narrow streets criss-crossed white.
It was a dream I fell in love with:
the attic, the double bed with you in it,
the aroma of coffee drifting up the stairs,
and me, moving away from the window
to slip silent as the snow in beside you
and dream of a love that was a trillion snowflakes
                                                            falling.

Remembering Palermo

I was in Palermo once,
in a room like this.

Each time,
after our lovemaking,

I would stand at the window and wonder
how we would be

when we returned to Taormina –
the tourists, the souvenir shops,

the less than authentic.
Everything appeared authentic

when we were in Palermo,
even our love,

which seemed fragile elsewhere,
felt more real there.

The breeze would blow the curtains into the room,
the smoke from your cigarette would enter my lungs,

and I would call to you to come,
and you always did, when we were in Palermo.

Had I Been Listening

I would have heard the door closing,
the small brass key turning the lock,
your soft retreating steps on the wet gravel.

I would have raised my head from
the warm hollow of my pillow, heard
the creek of the old double bed as I rose.

I would have stepped into the moonlit night,
carried you gently to our room,
placed your head back on your pillow.

It's simple, really:
I should have been listening.
I should have been paying attention.

Trust

Little by little trust crept back
but it had travelled such a distance
it could never return completely.

He knew this though she didn't.
She was oblivious to what was going on,
thought trust had never gone away.

He was going around in circles. Or,
he was at the end of a long cul-de-sac;
either way he didn't like where he was,

nor was he sure how he got there.
He had some idea (he was no fool),
but the extent of it bewildered him.

He was the type who liked a resolution.
He could see one up ahead,
though each time he approached, it receded.

Part of him guessed it would always be like this,
while another part prayed for it to stop.
The two parts went nowhere.

The delicate cross he wore around his neck,
said to produce miracles,
had failed to deliver any,

which made him wonder
if the cross was the problem.
That kind of muddled thinking

would get him nowhere,
which brought him back to the beginning,
where trust, or the lack of it, had come in.

What he Usually Did

It was what he usually did when the boat they were on
ran into a storm, or in this case floundered on the rocks:
he lay low and busied himself with tasks he had put off,
which goes a long way to explaining why he spent today
in a cold room with a can of paint and a brush in his hand.

He'd had a good feeling about the colour he had chosen.
Now that it's out of the tin and on the walls he is not so sure.
It brings a coldness to the room when it needed warmth.
It's a toss up whether she will ever see it. If their boat sinks,
which this time seems likely, she will send for her stuff.

Murphy's Law

I've been putting off writing this poem, especially here,
in this café, where an awkward encounter seems inevitable:
I will be here and you will enter
or
I will enter and you will be here.

It is a small world everywhere now.
Down here, in this watery town, it is smaller still,
a chance encounter unavoidable,
with me rambling these parts incessantly,
restless as always.

If I write the poem,
if I finally get the damn thing written,
Murphy's Law will be enacted for sure, with you
walking in the door just as I am closing it
one last, final time.

Letting Go

How the years have passed
since you first walked away from me
on a busy street and I followed you,
keeping the back of your head in sight
as the distance between us became greater,

until I lost you completely.

I think of you often, my love,
yet I also know this:
that even as I followed, we were letting go,
were already walking away,
though we had many miles to travel together.

STUPID

When I looked around there was only me,
and for a long time I would not accept
that you were not there to hold my hand
through thick and thin and all the rest of the shit

that gets thrown by people you thought you could trust.
I'd have to see this through alone,
the journey into oblivion,
my left hand clasping my right, and not yours,

as I had counted on, stupidly.

Elements

You will be in your element now,
clocking up impossibly long hours
and not a word about it,

covering all the angles,
the finishing touch just where it matters,
re-energized now that he's gone –

the big event and you at the heart of it.

He is in his own element,
solitary walks along a windswept Strandhill
that swallow up an hour or two

of these drearily long days without you.

Spinning

She was his centre of gravity,
so when she left, when she finally left,
he had nothing to keep him grounded,
only the memory of when they'd been together,
but memories alone were not enough
to prevent an unravelling, which was slow at first,
before picking up speed like a Hadron Collider.
By the end he was spinning like a spinning top,
spinning right off the face of the earth.
She went into the healing business
and may return in some enlightened future.
By then he will be in another galaxy,
beyond search and rescue,
a million light years beyond healing.

The Poems I Write Now

You never write me love poems, you once remarked.
The poems I write now set sail with no thoughts of you,

yet you always manage to climb on board
at the point where I am losing my way.

Apart from adrift, where that leaves me
I have no idea.

Looking Back

Looking back is a risky business;
I know it, yet I do it.

One day we will meet, face to face,
by chance, by accident, by ill luck.

I do not know how I will be,
other than lost for words,

lost for meaning,
lost all over again.

Picture This

Outside the window
the blue canvas of Roscommon sky
in the photograph on my kitchen counter
is dark and ominous as we descend into winter.

Inside
your image fades
as you walk through the long grass
into the fragile lens of that first summer.

Warrior of the Heart

We have entered the realm of the ridiculous.
There is no room for logic
where love gets in the way,
keeping us together when we should be apart.
Who of us can remember a time
when we were not bickering like bitter aunts?
You'll say the early years,
but they do not count, the early years:
we use those times to wander about
in the dizzying whirlpool of infatuation,
all the while biding our time.

You need a strong stomach
for our kind of heavy-duty jousting.
Mine was never well lined
and now you've turned it inside out.
That's the chance you take when you take on another;
it could be a good move, maybe your worst –
you won't know this side of Christmas,
but the truth will out in dribs and drabs
or in a great big whoosh
that'll have you running for your life,
the one you gave away in good faith to another.

I read a book about love once,
commanding me to be a warrior of the heart.
The best warriors are strong, brave, constant.
They know when to try a different line of attack,
when to retreat. Our fighting methods are instinctual.
We have no plans, no strategies. Our instruments are
crude and blunt and bludgeon the other with savage
indignation. Our listening skills in the heat of battle are so
poor we may as well be clinically deaf.

As our voices rise, our hearing diminishes.
I may as well be talking to the wall, we both say.

Last month we seemed close to achieving
some sort of peace on our small stage;
four days together and barely a ripple.
The flight home should have been an omen –
three hours late then the usual scramble
for a seat, two seats together,
for apart from anything else
you needed my hand to hold
through take-off, turbulence, shaky landing.
Where is your hand now?
Who are you holding on to?

I'm learning to live my life without you.
Day forty-four and it's going well, I think,
though any minute now I could be in the corner,
face turned to the wall,
wailing like the banshee on a bad day.
You're made of sterner stuff.
You say you are fragile
but I don't believe it.
I've seen you in action,
witnessed you going to battle.
You come from a long line of chieftains.

I will never leave you, you said,
and I thought you never would.
This is the most mature relationship
I've ever been in, I said, and I suppose

I must have swallowed it. We said many things,
made vows, deemed ourselves luckier than most.
Now we seem the most foolish of fools –
deluded, dismayed, silent for once.
We have run out of vows.
We have run out of time.
There is no one less dependable than us.

There'll be another stab at reconciliation
(we are nothing if not hopeless romantics).
The world will seem habitable again
as we celebrate our reincarnated life.
The dark will become light.
We will forget what comes next.
Then, out of the blue, it will happen,
blindsiding us back into battle.
We are prisoners of our sad merry-go-round,
killing ourselves slowly and we know it.
Time to call it a day, find hope in another dream.

Winter's Arrival

It did not rain today, though since morning
the wind has been warning the trees to brace themselves
for what is on the way. We have taken note.
We have secured the windows and lit the stoves.

The days ahead will be reliably grim.
Northerly winds will chill our bones.
This might be the winter the roof takes flight.
Hibernation will again seem an attractive proposition.

Still, it is worth repeating:
it did not rain today, though the wind did blow,
let's not forget that the wind blew through the tall trees
all through the late October day.

Connections

On a long, lonely road
I meet a man out cropping –
farmer's wellies, an old winter coat,
his daily kale, cabbage, sprouts.
We talk about his crop,
and, of course, the weather,

always the weather,
and the latest to die
an easy or a tragic death –
not the ice-breaker we need,
but it keeps us going,
keeps us connected.

We are two low-impact humans,
treading lightly on the earth,
understanding what makes a day bearable:
home-grown greens just picked,
a ride on a bicycle in the snow,
a neighbourly chat, a chance to laugh.

Our voices reclaim the past,
broad consonants settle in the snow,
hard syllables echo back at us
before rushing
like frightened animals
across the white meadows.

Glove

Don't let me ever lose these, she says,
handing them to me in the car park,
for the sea air is sharp and my hands are cold
and her dead father's gloves are a perfect fit.

The next morning I'm back again,
praying to Saint Anthony to find me a lost glove.
I peer over dune grass and into crevices,
make a fool's errand to a strip of tossed sea wrack.

Alas, much like Monty Python's parrot,
the glove is dead and isn't coming back.
And yet it does just that;
like a small miracle it is there,

in the boot of my car
that I have turned inside out
not once but five times
and one more time just in case.

I steer clear of miracles.
Before you know it every bloody thing
out of the ordinary is miraculous.
All I can say for certain is:

it was not there, and now here it is.

Mid-Points

About twenty years ago is my best guess,
give or take a few years either way.
That's assuming I'll avoid an encounter
with a tree on a bad bend
or any of the other life shorteners
hiding in the shadows.

My weekend city break had one too:
one-thirty Saturday afternoon, to be precise.
You were delayed – no surprise there –
thus missing the middle of my weekend,
though let's face it sweetheart,
you'll hardly stay the course,
which, come to think about it,
means we too may have passed
our very own mid-point.

What brought all this on?
Perhaps the thousands of Glasnevin tombstones
that rushed past the carriage window minutes ago,
or the cluttered rows of pale houses
stretching across what were once green fields
we played in when we were children,
or maybe it was the light covering of snow
on the distant Dublin Mountains
that brought about such unexpected sadness.

The Things they Say

They say I drove to Sligo today.
That must have been pleasant,
a soft winter Sunday,
wipers clearing the way.

They say I stopped in Strandhill,
that the tide was full,
that my takeaway espresso
hit the spot.

I must have driven home
because I am here now
after what they've said was
a nice day at the coast.

And now one final act
before the day is done:
this written record
to verify the fact.

On My 10th Birthday

I am the golden apple of my father's eye,
I am crying again and I don't know why.

I am my sister's gentle and tender brother,
I am too fragile for this world says my mother.

I am sunshine and sweetness and light,
I am invisible all day and all night.

Those Wives

Time speeds up the older you get
said those old wives who had no watches.

Those wives knew a thing or two,
and not just about runaway time.
They knew how to raise a dozen children,
how to run a tight ship, how to steer a course
through the moods of the men they married.
I could have done with a wife like that,
she might have softened my edges,
helped me live a less rigid life.
All my life I've been making lists:
January plans mapping out my future,
daily to-dos to keep the engine running.
Now might be a good time
to slow this vintage model down,

take the foot off the pedal,
relax into the downhill slide.

His Women

His memory has failed him,
his remarkable life out of reach.
The women who no longer love him
are lost forever in a permanent shadow.
There's one of them now, at the next table.
She catches his eye, nods in fond remembrance.
He smiles to let her know she is still in his thoughts.

Poetry and Physiotherapy

Inside the café the poets hunker down,
united in their bad posture.

It's a pressure cooker
where creative juices overheat,

abandoned cappuccinos cool,
minds are bent and stretched.

The physio, morning coffee break over,
hikes back across the hunched bridge.

She has left her card on the counter
for the mindbenders with the backaches.

Artifice

Ironically,
when it came down to it,
what failed him every time were words.

He awoke
on that first day of renewal
to a bare table, two notebooks, a pencil and a dictionary.

He wrote a word in one notebook,
began a poem in another, which he titled 'Artifice',
and he deemed it a reasonable start, all things considered.

Silent

He suspected it might be over,
there seemed to be nothing there,
not an original thought forthcoming.

He wondered was it age,
lack of stimulation,
an absence of drama.

Drama had been at the heart of the last effort,
and the misery and depression that followed.
Not that he wished for their return,

nor the sickness that floored him after.
The misery was good for what it dragged out of him
but he would rather be silent than pay a return visit.

He would be silent so –
which could bring its own misery.

The Competition

Miles away, on the other side of the country,
a rival poet, brightest of them all,
was launching.

Of course he went;
to support,
to be seen to support.

He was generous to a fault,
thoroughly engaged,
and threatened.

On the long drive back
he was in composition overdrive,
fuelled by the luminosity of the competition.

This Foolishness

Sometimes the penny drops
and all I can do to keep me sane
is stop this foolishness, put down the pen,
shrug on a coat and walk through the meadow
and into the woods where the trees stand waiting always.

When All is Said and Done
i.m. Dennis O'Driscoll

When all is said and done,
the one poem that always gets to me
is that six-liner by Dennis O'Driscoll
about the bath,
and the pizza he never got to enjoy.

When all is said and done
reminds me of a song my mother sang
towards the end of parties
when the gin had kicked in
and she took to the floor.

When all is said and done
is a neat little phrase you can slot
into a poem just like this,
because when all is said and done
no one will notice.

When all is said and done,
someone will phone to tell you
the ambulance is on its way
right now
to where you thought you were standing.

Ailbhe

> the spider's genius
> to spin and weave in the same action
> from her own body, anywhere –
> even from a broken web.
> – 'Integrity', Adrienne Rich

I will nursery-rhyme you into their world,
spin a tale of patience and entrapment,
weave their wondrous ways into your open soul
so you will feel tenderness towards them
because they are just as much a part of our universe
as you are, sweetheart, curled up in your dream world.

16TH OCTOBER

1

You were still warm when I touched you
as you lay on your back in the hospital morgue.
Later, I thought about all your warm embraces,
and how you had held back the cold until I got there.

2

I have no memory of turning off the cooker
though I must have done, for the flat was dark and cold
when I returned hours later
rudderless
motherless
the answerphone blinking red
out of synch with my heartbeat in the darkness.

Inner City

It's an early morning start for our local street beggar.
He holds with dark brown hands a paper cup,
offers it like a gift to his reluctant customers.
They wait, poised for the green,
the race to beat the red at the top of the hill.
One by one he wears them down, bar those
who have a thing about the colour of his skin,
who'd spit in his migrant face
if they could get away with it.
The beggar has seen them all. He has learned to ignore
the meanness and the abuse,
the compassion and the kindness.
He is, it is true, a little unhinged. He berates himself,
has protracted arguments with his shadow.
He is our morning alarm, rousing the street
with his plaintive, Bedouinesque cry.

Casablanca

Kindness came to him begrudgingly,
an unexpected offering
from the warehouse of cynicism
that were his bricks and mortar.

His instinct was to mock,
undermine, diminish:
a preference for a book derided,
an opinion dismissed with a sigh.

He knew when he had gone too far.
He could be Rick in *Casablanca* then,
a study in despair – minus the charisma –
staring at the floor.

A new subject would be floated.
For a while there would reside
an unnatural calmness in the room
that he could hardly bear.

The Master

His early calling long on the wane,
the Master beats the table with his cane.
His charges are a room of thirty-six:
he batters them with ash and hazel sticks.

RING

My mother, God bless her, gave me a ring.
I'd have preferred something to eat,
a hard cheese to last a long journey,
a square of bread, even,
but there was no food in the cottage,
which is why we were all of us leaving.

Now the ring is gone, slipped off my finger
during the mayhem of the last hour,
the pushing and the jostling on the pier,
the scramble onto deck. I lost it then,
when I flung that woman to the ground,
the one who tried to steal my place

on this wreck of a boat they call a ship,
which must be some kind of joke.
I've spent my life on the water
and this spent vessel will not, I fear,
be up to what we are about to do:
cross an ocean to a new life.

The woman I threw to the ground,
she has my mother's ring, I am sure of it,
she will have seen its dull sheen on the pier,
will have slipped it onto her finger.
She is the fortunate one,
if you can call a condemned woman fortunate.

She has dry land to die on.
I have an ocean waiting to take me.

Freedom

Against the odds you made it happen,
despite the advice of those
who thought you foolish and impetuous,
delusional or just plain mad.
You didn't bend. You didn't falter.
Now here you are in the flush of landing,
amazed you've reached this moment,
for only now can you see
the layers of entrapment peeling away,
only now can you feel
the wings you knew were there
shift against your shoulder blades.

Lockdown

This is where we are,
where we have washed up,
our final resting place.

There is no turning back.
We must learn to be still,
to observe this earthly paradise

unfold
in every common flower,
in every blessèd tree,

in every scent,
in every sound,
in every breath.

Acknowledgements

Thanks to Roscommon County Council for residency bursaries at the Tyrone Guthrie Centre in Annaghmakerrig; to the management and staff at Annaghmakerrig, where many of the poems in this collection were redrafted and finalised; to all the poets with whom I have had the pleasure and privilege of working, especially those gifted poets in Roscommon, Leitrim and Sligo. I have learned more from them than they have learned from me.

Finally, a huge debt of gratitude to my publisher, Alan Hayes at Arlen House, for his ongoing support of so many writers, and for producing so many wonderful books over the years.

About the Author

Gerry Boland is a Dublin-born writer of poetry and prose. He writes for adults and for children and has published ten books to date. He was Writer-in-Residence for Roscommon County Council in 2013 and 2014 and he continues to work in an advisory capacity on the county's annual Literary Development Programmes. He runs regular creative writing workshops, both in-person and online, and he also provides a mentoring service to emerging writers. He lives in rural north Roscommon.

OTHER BOOKS BY GERRY BOLAND

The Far Side of Happiness (Arlen House, 2018), short fiction
The Secret Lives of Mothers (author, 2017), children's poetry
In the Space Between (Arlen House, 2016), poetry
Marco Moonwalker (O'Brien Press, 2012), children/YA
Marco Master of Disguise (O'Brien Press, 2012), children/YA
Watching Clouds (Doghouse, 2011), poetry
Marco Moves In (O'Brien Press, 2011), children/YA
Stroller's Guide to Dublin (Gill&Macmillan, 1999), non-fiction
A Dublin Pocket Guide (Aer Lingus, 1994), non-fiction